STORY 400

ARAMI WALKER

Introduction

Story 400 is a collection of poetry written by writer and musician, Arami Walker. In August 2019, she began writing this book at 25 years old with the intention of reflecting on history and modernity. In 1619, the first group of African people were taken to North America. 400 years later, Walker reflects on 1/12 of this historical timeline with roots in Africa and Europe. Her reflections are on love, progress, trauma, celebration, ecology, music, history, and the promise for tomorrow.

I found these lyrics and poems in the midst of transformation, a global pandemic, struggle, fear, joy, love, and deep introspection.

In the years to come, I hope we all remember who we are and the importance of our intimate communities and the environment.

In honor and dedication for all those who allowed me the opportunity to exist and thrive, this is for you.

STORY 400

STORY 400

For our ancestors, words by a modern woman.

Story 400

Four hundred years past-
You do not own our bodies.
This is our story.

08-26-2019

Cotton and sugar
So pure and white, fueled slavery.
Black hands bled daily.

08/29 /2019

STORY 400

Process your Anger.
Compelled by an illusion
Trapped by fixation.

09/07/2019
*inspired by J.P

Conscious, true, healing-
Unraveling history
Together we rise.

09-10-2019
*inspired by N.U

Mother is Talking,
She speaks of hands touching soil.
Hear her, hear her now!

09/08/2019
*Inspired by J.G

A diversity-
Plants, animals, fungus, bugs
creates fertile soil.

10-06-2019

Deep Breath- In and out.
Meditation is our Hope
To consciously Heal.

09/02/2019

Therapy is key-
Oh to have someone listen.
You are not alone.

Pacific Northwest
Innovation and Compost-
Who would have thought so?

12/16/2019
*inspired by A.M

Masculinity-
Strong, bold, fierce, powerful Man.
Love females, wholly.

10-22-2019

Femininity-
Soft, graceful, pristine, beauty.
Get back in rhythm.

10-24-2019

Water, Air, Earth, Light-
Connect body, mind, and soul.
We only have now.

10-03-2019

One Language limits
Experience and world view-
Welcome something new!

09/06/2019
*Inspired by S.G

Breathing is our right!
Do not privatize the air,
We have one planet.

10/07/2019

Absent mother's keep
Sunflowers face the sun, yet
Strive, straight root to stalks.

09/11/2019
*Written by my father for his mother.

Reconnect when whole,
You won't find yourself in them.
Self love then real love.

09/23/2019

New year grass in snow-
The Ox will plow this year's crop.
We have persevered.

*Ox New year's Eve 2021

Improvisation-
Jazz, rhythm, poetry, and blues
Got us through it all.

09/212019

We must redefine
Love for our generation-
Balance must be found.

10/11/2019

Time is a triplet-
A rhythmic continuum,
Past, present, future.

09/12/2019
*inspired by J.P and B.M

Arts Activism-
We need to CREATE, a new
Music industry.

10/15/2019
*inspired by S.S

In your eyes, I see
A version of me complete-
My sweet Melody.

09/14/2019

Healing takes a while-
Be patient and flexible.
We will recover.

09/19/2019

Towering Sky High
Reaching for my Dreams, blast-off
That's right, I can Fly.

09/05/2019
*Written by my father

STORY 400

You deserve Real Love-
Don't give up, just be patient.
The answer will come.

04/05/2020

Bread rising slowly
Feeding the community
Warmth and nutrition.

10/14/2019
*inspired by J.L

Intention is key-
Balance can be created.
Seeds will be planted.

09/17/2019

Loyalty and trust
Resilience and Strong Friendship,
What we all long for.

10/12/2019

I like being alone.
I like being with my friends.
I need both to live.

10/25/2019

Unpack each sentence-
Dogma revealed in secret.
Where does the truth lie?

09/28/2019

Cycle of Power-
Sometimes you need to turn off
So you can reset.

09/15/2019

Do not fear yourself!
Anger is information.
What is she saying?

10/01/2019

Stay healthy and fit-
Show me smart and show me strength.
Bring a friend for fun.

10/23/2019

Liberation comes
When we unite and resist-
We are resilient.

08/30/2019

Indigenous folks
And farmers are suffering-
Stop Monocropping!

10/05/2019

Love in their language-
Affirmation, gifts, service,
Quality time, touch.

09/24/2019

*Inspired by The Five Love Languages: How to Express Heartfelt Commitment to Your Mate by Gary Chapman.

Story 400

So much Art to be made-
Times when I am overwhelmed
Relax and Do it!

01/08/2020

Velvet Voices sing,
harmonizing with the wind-
Forgive, don't forget!

09/03/2019

Absent Mindedness-
I pick up my scattered thoughts,
Mosaic of me.

10/18/2019

Take a break sometimes,
You can't do it all right now!
It will come in time.

09/18/2019

Do not give up please,
Mindset is the key, now breathe.
Put your mind in place.

09/29/2019

A Female Leader
Is necessary to heal
Male inflicted wounds.

08/31/2019

The Liberator-
A newspaper fuels freedom.
Abolished hatred.

09/26/2019

Help each other shine,
Together we climb, fearless
Is our state of mind.

09/16/2019

Climate change is here-
We need fertile soil, clean air,
And the will to change.

10/04/2019

Take a break from screens-
Social media and Ads
Can make you hate you.

10/02/2019

I am not the past
I am not the future, no
I am this moment.

01/04/2021

It's time to sing songs-
To dance the rhythm of life
We belong, we do.

04/07/2021

Story 400

I am black and white-
A true unification.
Welcome, new generations.

04/07/2021

Find peace from within-
I am a whole universe
I am a whole self.

04/07/2021

Entrepreneur
Black female empowerment-
Madame C Walker

04/07/2021

Whole self and whole self-
Two complete human beings
Enjoying our time.

04/07/2021

Revitalized mind-
Acknowledging history
Without the burden.

04/08/2021

PART TWO
A Brighter Future

A UNIVERSE BY NATURE

Painting by: J.Prouty Under

Aquarius

Love is like the ocean
And she wipes away my fear-
Through the pain we take our steps
So we can persevere.

I feel it in my heart and soul
I know our time is near,
Love is like the ocean and she wipes away my tears.

But how can I love anyone else before I love myself?
How can I love anyone else?
How can I love love anyone else before I love myself?
How can I love anyone else?

Walking in your footsteps, I see symbols in the sand
Grab a pen and paper let your words flow through my hand-
I feel it in my heart and soul
We've reached the promised land
Everything you've done has made me everything I am.

But how can I love anyone else before I love myself?
How can I love anyone else?
How can I love love anyone else before I love myself?
How can I love anyone else?

Catalyze catharsis in my body, mind, and soul
never know what's coming so you got to let it go
To the flow or the whole of eternity
Just wait and see, just wait and see.

Be like water
And go with the flow-
With the flow.

I'm a template
For a temple-
Not simple.
Complex-
Grab a pencil
No stencil.
Freehand
Instrumental-
No samples.
Freestyle
You just ramble,
get trampled.
Stampede
In the land fool-
Don't gamble.
Words hot
Like the mantle-
Get cancelled.
Won't change for the man
No,
I am who I am so.

But how can I love anybody else before I love myself?
How can I love anybody else before I love myself?

I will always go with the flow,
 I'll always take it real-
I'll always take it real, slow.

Real Slow, Slow, Slow.

Obsidiana

Overcoming the darkness and the hollow confines of insecurity.

No tengo tiempo para energía negativa.
No tengo tiempo para energía negativa
No tengo tiempo para energía negativa.
No tengo tiempo para energía negativa

(I don't have time for negative energy.)

Ahora es mi tiempo yo lo sé-
El destino es lo que yo manifesté
Y yo se que a veces es difícil
Pero, yo voy a superar lo que necesito.

(Right now is my time, I know it.
My destiny is what I manifested
And I know that sometimes it gets hard,
But I will overcome everything I need to overcome.)

I just have to let it go, let it flow
I just want to be whole again.
I just want to see through all the see through people around you-
(El camino es así)

I just need some transparency,
I just want to find a way to reach my destiny.
Leave the past, in the past
(if it doesn't spark joy no more)
And I liberate myself so I can see.

With my third eye,
And in between the lines I find like-
Red, orange, yellow, green, purple, white light
ignites the insight, the clarity.

(I want to liberate my mind and soul)
Speaking only verities, speaking on verities .

Press rewind.

Siento con mi corazón y alma
El pensamiento es como un río, en mi mente
Algo para la gente en Sudamérica.
Sobreviviendo-
contra, todo lo que necesitamos
Luchar.

(I feel with my heart and soul
Thoughts are a river in my mind
This one is for the people in South America
Surviving everything we need to, fight.

I don't have time for negative energy
I don't have time for negative energy)

Ahora es el tiempo,
Ahora es el espacio
Para superar
Todo lo que necesito para
Liberarme
Para
(I got to find a way to be whole again)
Llegar a mi sueño.

(*Now is the time*
Now is the space
To overcome everything necessary in order to liberate myself
In order to arrive at my dream)

No tengo tiempo, no tengo tiempo, para energía negativa.
(We always make it through)

Adelante-
Con familia y amor.

(I don't have time for negative energy
Forward with family and love.)

Simple Gifts

The sun, the sky, the rain-
The tea, the food, the music that we play
The love, the light, the trust, the loyalty-

These are the simple things.
These are the simple gifts of life, of time.

Oh, the simple gift of life

And I know that I will get by every time-
and I go to sleep at night
knowing that I tried.
I won't give up this time-
No, I won't give up this time around.

I know when I'm feeling down
I got to rise up off the ground-
I know my time is coming soon
and I will make it, I will make it through
Because I got you, I got you.

And that is the simple gift of life.

Oh, the simple gift of time.

The sun, the stars, the sky, the moon, the water, the food, the friends, the love, the light, the trust-

These are simple gifts of life.

This song is dedicated to my father and all the men who uplift me.

Breathe again

I am learning how to breathe
I am learning how to breathe.
The moment I came to this world
I knew my breath was all I needed.

I'm tired of searching for love-
I'm tired of obsessing over my own delusions,
My own illusions, I just want to breathe.
I Just want to breathe.

Breathe into the lungs of life
Breathe into my soul,
Breathe until the pain subsides,
Breathe until you're whole.

Let the Love flow into your soul
Let the Love flow into your soul
Let the Love flow into your soul
Let the Love flow into your soul
And Breathe.

Painting by: B.Mamani
Photo by: V.Zarate

Mercury ST.

Sometimes life is moving really fast, around me-
Let go of all the burdens of the past, that bound me.

Chakras aligned catch my momentum-
Moe on the track equals mo' income
Win some, invest in my family income.
Celebrate with hao chi
Order dim sum.
Win some, mutually invested like ETF stock funds
Don't run, from the sum of words that you have to say.

(Overcompensating when I'm feeling frustrated)

Another day around the sun, what's done is done.
For better outcomes don't run.
For better outcomes don't run,
From the sum, of words you have to say
We're blessed to see another day.
We're blessed to see another day.

Sometimes, life is moving really fast, around me.
Let go-
of all the burdens of the past, that bound me.
Let go
Let go.

We're protected by the music
we protect it and we use it.
To reflect and keep you grooving, show respect cause this a movement.
(Sometimes life is moving really fast, around me)
Show respect because this is a movement.

We are the keepers of time,
And the time is, and the time is, and the time is

Now.

Deep rooted

This is a hypnotic meditation-
Positive vibration, elation,
This a sensation.
Waiting until I come up-
Words that sum up
The Indifference
Of you and me-
I, equality
I just want to see
Eye to eye
So you can realize
The mask of masculinity-
The disguise you were born into-
But your mindset is up to you.
Hopefully you make it through
That is persistence, this is resistance
Wondering who this is
Searching for myself in door ways, hallways, condos, apartments with keys-
Singing songs that bring you to your knees
I just want to breathe.
I just want to breathe.

I just want to breathe.
I just want to breathe.

And I am not afraid to say no-
Just so you know,
I am not a monkey nor a hoe.
Where's my dough?

Bread rose an hour ago
So we break it-
Make not mistake this Wit

was designed to illuminate the state with
Elevated consciousness.

I'm sick of all the nonsense in
Media, hysteria, criteria not innocuous.
My words are inconspicuous,
A mystery to the sophist's list of ideology
What's their reasoning for reconnaissance?

Are you feeling this?
Are you feeling this?

It goes deep.

Only you can free your mind.

And when your walking through the valley of darkness alone-
I hope you find yourself.
Deeper, deeper in your self awareness-
Thoughts from before and after you
coming to this moment.

I hope you move forward in life, in 2020 vision,
Humanity rising together.
Masculinity and femininity working together-
To uplift us to a better situation.

Partnerships that are real, founding in love and loyalty,
what is your love language so I can see-
how to bring myself to the highest level to meet you,
because we as people deserve to love.

Structure of water

Hey,

I just want to make things right-

Stay and I won't go
But if you leave...

Stay and I won't go
But if you have to go...

People come and people go
Like the tides it ebbs and flows.

Life is a circle-
Some hands you hold and some you have to let go.

Stay and I won't go
Stay and I won't go

But if you have to leave...

Stay and I won't go
But if you have to leave...

I can't keep running away.
I can't keep running away.

It's the circle of life.

People come and people go
Like the tides it ebbs and flow.

Life is a circle,
Some hands you hold, some you have to let go.

Stay and I won't go
Sometimes we rise,
sometimes we fall.

And there's such a thing as too much of a good thing.
Sometimes we rise, sometimes we fall.

I can't keep running away.

Sometimes we rise
Sometimes we fall.
It's the circle of life, you know.
Let us hold you, skin like Earth-

Remember our worth,
Remember our worth.

Healing song

Unraveling, so much
Feeling in our bodies and soul.
Conscious, true, healing for-
all the pain we feel in our bodies
Let it go.

Shake off the demons in our minds,
and our souls.

Ah, soul.
I promise to love myself,
If you love yourself too.
I promise to heal myself
If you heal yourself too.
I promise to love myself
If you love yourself too.
I promise to heal myself
If you heal yourself, too.

I promise to-
Heal myself if you heal yourself too.

The female body-
Men, let us hold you
Sink into our skin, like your feet on the earth
Do you remember our worth?

Respect me and I will respect you too.
Love me and I will love you too.
I am because of you.
I am because of you.

Ubuntu (I am because You are)

I am because of you and you are because of me too.
I am the sun and you are the moon-
I am the spring and you are the flower that blooms.
I will wait for you,
I will always be true.
I am because of you, and you are because of me too.

Hold me in your arms I want to stay-
Awakened from our dream don't run away.
Because real love,
Baby it comes with time-
and I know that we will be alright.

Because I am because of you
And you are because of me too.

Because of me, too.
Because of me, too.

And I will always, always love you.

Through the good and the bad, through the beautiful
Through the painful, through the storm.

Because I am because of you,
And you are because of me too.

Respect Freestyle

Respect
Respect
Respect

Now we are respecting each other,
Sisters and brothers
learning how to love.
Love each other-
Men loving women, women loving men,
and all the in between.

I just want to find a song to sing, this is improvised poetry-
straight from our hearts, straight from our souls
I just want to let you know, I just want to let you know
that I respect you,
And I need you to respect me too.

Respect, can I get some love in the building.

Respect your mama.

It's all love in here.
It's all love in here
It's all respect, never forget, this is a classic.
This is a classic.

This is me

Well you have to be different,
but in a beautiful way.
Well you have to be stronger,
with all the words that they say.

I am not afraid
no, I am not afraid
to be exactly what
I'm meant to be-
This is me.

This is me.

Fighting for our place in society
Living oh, so quietly.
Making music so vividly,
Can't you see we are his dream?
This is me, this is me, this is me
and I feel so alive.
So, alive.

Vamos caminando, Vamos
Vamos caminando, siguiendo la verdad.
(*Lets go walking, Lets go.*
Lets go walking, seeking the truth.)

This is me, This is me, This is me,

And we are free, free, free.

Worth The Wait

Day turns to night
Turns to life
Turns to memories-
Pass by,
Like the clouds
In the sky, flying high.

Oh, I learn to wait
For my fate
For my sake.
Oh, I learn to wait
For my fate
For my sake.

Because good things, they come with time
You'll find.

That good things, they come with time,
You'll find.

So I'll learn to wait, for my fate
For my sake.
I'll learn to wait, for my fate
For my sake.

Because good things,
They come with time
You'll find.
That good things
They come with time
You'll find.

My destiny is unfolding right in front of me
I can't believe that it's finally happening

Until I came here today, finally found my way.

Because good things,
They come with time
You'll find.
That good things
They come with time
You'll find.

I'll learn to wait for my fate, for my sake
Cause good things they come with time.

Thank you to my parents, grandparents, sisters, brothers, band, teachers, and students.

A better future-
We are in this together.
Ad Infinitum.

www.ingramcontent.com/pod-product-compliance
Lightning Source LLC
Chambersburg PA
CBHW072017290426
44109CB00018B/2266